# The finest plants for the garden

HERMIEN VAN WIJHE-RUYS

REBO
PRODUCTIONS

© 1997 Rebo Productions b.v., The Netherlands
© 1997 Published by Rebo Productions Ltd.
text: Hermine van Wijhe-Ruys
cover design: Ton Wienbelt, The Netherlands
photographic editor: Marieke Uiterwijk
editor: Renske de Boer, TextCase, The Netherlands
layout: Signia, The Netherlands
type-setting: Hof&Land Typografie, The Netherlands

ISBN 1 901094 758

# Contents

# Preface

Gardening is a wonderful hobby which can rapidly take over your life if you have a large country garden. What could be more delightful after a busy day than cultivating the soil – at least, that's how I feel. Apart from tending the garden, just looking at things is a joy: looking to see what is coming up, looking at the plants' beautiful shapes, and at their lovely colours and combinations of colours. There are different flowers and new colours to admire in every season. Even in winter, when there appears to be nothing in the garden at all, it's wonderful to discover that even then there are plants and shrubs with something special about them.

Garden lovers will find some information on all kinds of 'old' and 'new' plants in this book. You will read about details such as unusual (leaf) shapes and fine colours, and whether the plant is easy to grow, or more suitable for experienced gardeners.

The colour photographs will give you some ideas on how to combine plants. Most of them were taken in gardens and nurseries in The Netherlands, and a few in National Trust and private gardens in Britain.

The plants, trees and shrubs described in this book are suitable for average-sized gardens. They are also adapted to fairly cool climates. I know of some gardeners who spend the entire winter protecting their valuable favourites from the cold. Frost-tender plants that need protection in winter have not been included in this book.

Hermine van Wijhe-Ruys

Left: Pontederia cordata

Right: Rosa 'Annie M.G. Schmidt'

# The nomenclature of plants

The Netherlands, like Britain, is very much a land of gardens, and many developments in gardening are taking place there. Dutch growers have a good reputation in other countries, and in Britain and France I regularly come across plants grown in The Netherlands. Dutch gardens can certainly vie with those in Britain.

Chrysanthemum carinatum 'Kokarde'

Right: Formal design in the gardens of Wijlre Castle, The Netherlands.

Gardens in The Netherlands are full of surprises. The modern garden is a mixture of styles, from the free and natural English designs to the more formal layouts of the 'jardin à la française', and new ideas like those of Mien Ruys.

For the plant trade as well as for science, it is vitally important for plants to be known by the same names everywhere. No one in Britain, for example, would know what to do with 'cat's tails', a name used only in The Netherlands. Plants are therefore often referred to by their Latin names. This Latin nomenclature can be difficult and rather annoying for up-and-coming gardeners, but it is really not too bad once you have become accustomed to it.

Linnaeus, the great Swedish botanist, laid the foundations for the present binomial nomenclature. He had a huge collection of plants, which he classified on the basis of brief descriptions.

*Cleen Lelie Garden in Oostvoorne, The Netherlands.*    *Rural garden in Domburg, The Netherlands.*

He published his *Species plantarum*, in which he included over 15,000 plants, in 1753. Each plant was given two names (binomial nomenclature): one for the genus, and one for the species. Plants with similar characteristics – especially structural features relating to the number of petals, the stamens, and the arrangement of leaves on the stem – were given the same generic name, for instance *Incarvillea*.

The names adopted by Linnaeus were based on Latin or Greek. They were often derived from the name of a botanist, a Greek mythological character, or some other person who had contributed to botanical knowledge. *Incarvillea*, for example, comes from d'Incarville, a French missionary in China, who collected native plants and sent them to Europe. In the world of plants, these generic names always begin with a capital. The second names indicate the various species

Oenothera biennis

Above: Hydrangea arborescens 'Annabelle'

Below: garden in The Netherlands, shows how a white garden may be very beautiful.

*Above:* Lythrum salicaria *combined with* Juncus inflexus. *The common names of these two plants are purple loosestrife and rush.*

*Left: The common name of* Nicandra physalodes *is apple of Peru.*

*Right:* Delphinium 'Rosy Future'

and often describe differences between them. *Incarvillea delavayi* is one of many examples. This second name always begins with a small letter, and may also be derived from a person, as in *delavayi*. Delavayi was another French missionary in China as well as a botanist. The second name may also be based on one of the plant's characteristics, for instance: *niger, nigrum* = black, as in *Veratrum nigrum*. Common epithets of this kind include the following: *albus* meaning white; *purpureus* or *purpurascens* purple; *ruber* red; *variegatus* variegated; *pendulus* pen-

dent; *fastigiatus* columnar; and *rectus* erect. In this way you can find out something about a plant without having seen it. *Veronica virginica* 'Rosea', for example, was probably first discovered in Virginia (USA). The epithet 'Rosea' refers to the pink colour of the flowers. There may also be *culti*vated *var*ieties, or cultivars, of some plants. That name begins with a capital and is printed in inverted commas, for example *Salvia officinalis* 'Tricolor'. A cultivar is a plant which

*Left:* Allium giganteum, *giant allium*

*Right:* Leptandra *'Virginica'*

*Below:* Platycodon grandiflorum, *the balloon flower*

Veronica virginica 'Rosea' is a tall plant that bears pink
flowers from July to September.

Salvia officinalis 'Tricolor' is a medicinal plant (officinalis) with
tri-coloured leaves.

*Previous pages:* Astilbe 'Bremen'

differs from the species as a result of hybridization, or of sowing and selecting forms found in
the wild.

To make things even more complicated, varieties
of plants may also occur. Again, the plant has
three names, but the last one is not printed in

inverted commas and does not begin with a capital, for example *Euphorbia amygdaloides* var.
*robbiae.*

A variety of a plant differs from the species because of, for example, climatic changes, or differences in soil or height. When you sow varieties,

Euphorbia amygdaloides *var.* robbiae *is an evergreen plant
that will tolerate a shady location. The plant develops suckers,
which makes it suitable for underplanting.*

Crocosmia masonorum

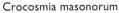

the ultimate appearance of the flowers will depend on the provenance of the seed.

Like Linnaeus, Charles Darwin was mainly engaged in studying similarities between families and genera. Darwin wrote that various plants resemble one another because they have common ancestors.

Both scientists were largely concerned with seeking connections; they were less interested in the various hybrids. Gardening enthusiasts, on the other hand, take particular note of the external features of the various mutations.

Ligularia stenocephala *'The Rocket'*

*Below:* Veronica prostrata

# CHAPTER 2

# Thoughts on planting

Most people think of perennials as the most important plants to grow; they are the very essence of a garden. They do not require as much care as annuals and, once a border has been planted out properly, groups of plants growing close together can keep weeds to a minimum. One drawback to perennials is that they sometimes proliferate and become invasive. Growers have tried to suppress such tendencies by means of hybridization, and this has proved successful in some cases.

*Border in Cleen Lelie Gardens.*

Perennials fill a garden with colour, almost all the year round if selected carefully. Although the available assortment has increased considerably, neighbouring gardens frequently still contain the same species of plants. Unfortunately, there are still some gardeners who divide the plants in one garden only to sell the surplus to the neighbours. It is important for perennials to be planted in such a way that they feel at home in a particular location and in a particular kind of soil. The fact is that not all plants have the same requirements: some thrive in heavy soil, whereas other prefer a lighter type.

It is quite satisfactory to grow plants that flower at the same time close together; the garden looks

*Left:* Salvia nemorosa *'Amethyst' is a handsome plant for a border.*

*Below:* Houttuynia cordata *'Chamaeleon' is a perennial with magnificent leaves.*

The lilac-pink Monarda *'Beauty of Cobham' likes a nutritive border. Its dark foliage is aromatic.*

*Next pages:* Limonium latifolium *thrives in heavier types of soil. This splendid sea lavender has shiny oblong leaves and bears strong, branching clusters of flowers, which keep their appeal when dried.*

much more attractive if two or more kinds of plant are in flower simultaneously. It is preferable not to plant one particular species dotted around in various parts of the garden, as that creates a rather patchy look.

## *Annuals*

These are plants which are sown in spring, flower in summer, and die down in autumn. They are spendid for filling gaps and producing instant effects. It is possible, for instance, to plant them

Lysimachia ephemerum *(foreground, white) and* Veronica longifolia *(blue).*

tumn, they may be moved to the spot where they are to flower the following spring. They will then die down at the end of that season. They usually produce quite a lot of seeds, so they will not disappear once they have died, and, in fact, you will usually have more of them in your garden the following year.

They often flower so early that it does not matter at all if they proliferate. Just think of violas, honesty, or forget-me-nots – all of them lovely to look at in spring.

*Right:* Astrantia, *masterwort, does not do equally well in all types of soil. In this photograph, it looks very attractive with* Digitalis *(foxglove) and* Lychnis, *a combination suitable for any border.*

*Next pages: A multi-coloured border consisting mainly of annuals.*

*Below:* Phlox cornuta *'Miss Lindgard'*

in spots where perennials refuse to grow because it is too dark there. Another advantage of annuals is that there are so many different ways of growing them. They are suitable for pots or other containers on a patio or in the garden. They are easy to cultivate, either by sowing seeds under cover early in the year, or by sowing them directly where they are to flower later on. Include a few special foliage plants such *Ricinus communis*, the castor-oil plant, which is suitable for a warm position, or the magnificent grey-leafed *Senecio bicolor* ssp. *Cineraria*.

## Biennials

Biennials should be sown in June/July. Once they have developed a rosette of leaves in au-

Biennials also include great many summer-flowering plants. You are bound to find some of the following in most gardens: foxgloves, mullein, moth mullein and hollyhocks.

Planting them in groups will lead to a grand display of colour.

## *Trees*

Even an average-sized garden needs a tree or two. Trees, after all, have always played a major part in human lives. Justice was administered under oak trees long ago. People used to believe that some trees were inhabited by gods, and that certain trees stood guard over a village or region.

*Left: Lavatera 'Barnsley' (pink)*

*Below: With its low, rounded crown, this Japanese maple, Acer palmatum, is an excellent tree for a garden, primarily because it does not grow too tall and may really be planted anywhere. It does, however, require some protection against very cold east winds.*

Trees are major producers of oxygen, and life is impossible without trees. Cutting down trees, old ones in particular, should therefore be avoided. Simple arithmetic will show that a beech tree, 25 metres (80 feet) tall, with a crown measuring 15 metres (50 feet) in diameter, will produce as much oxygen as 2500 youthful beech trees.

Give some serious thought to the matter before deciding to plant a tree – you will avoid a great deal of misery in that way. Just remember all those huge trees planted too close to windows and shutting out far too much light from the house.

Trees and shrubs are important for the structure

*Right: Mullein or* Verbascum blattaria *is a biennial that self-seeds extensively. That is not much of a problem, as the plant is not unduly invasive.*

*Below: Medlars,* Mespilus germanica, *photographed here in a garden in Nisse. The fruit is eaten when overripe.*

of a garden, especially in winter when the plants have died down.

Gardens would be bare indeed without trees or shrubs.

A tree may also be an important feature in a garden during other seasons. A tree in the foreground may give a small garden a greater appearance of depth, and there are more of these simple tricks in which trees play a part. Trees are important to birds, which build their nests in them. Trees also provide delightfully shady spots in the garden at the height of summer.

*Left: Prunus subhirtella 'Autumnalis', shown here with Geranium macrorrhizum as underplanting, is a tree shaped like a shrub. It bears pale pink flowers.*

*Below: This salmon-coloured hollyhock is not long-lived. Collecting its seeds will ensure that it does not disappear.*

Magnolia soulangeana *is a familiar tree, often incorrectly called tulip tree.*

Columbines (Aquilegia) *and apples* (Malus) *make an unusual combination.*

*Below: This magnificent deciduous* Viburnum carlesii, *native to Korea among other places, bears fragrant flowers in April/May.*

## Shrubs

Nearly all the properties of trees also apply to shrubs. Although they are usually smaller than trees, they still provide a structure for the garden and opportunities for birds to nest in them. The

*During severe winters, the roots of* Ceanothus delileanus *'Gloire de Versailles' should be kept covered, for instance with pine branches.*

*Below: This photograph shows how shrubs add structure to a garden.*

difference between trees and shrubs in based on the stem or stems: unlike a tree, which first forms a single stem, a shrub emerges from the soil with several small stems. In most instances, a shrub looks best at eye level, whereas you have to look high above you for a good view of a tree.

As soon as you plant a few shrubs, your garden will gain some features. Shrubs are often used for hedging purposes, and if you have enough space, that is infinitely preferable to a fence made of dead material.

Shrubs can be either evergreen or deciduous. The evergreen species retain their leaves throughout the year, and form a good contrast with deciduous shrubs, which herald the changing seasons. Try to achieve a balance between evergreen and deciduous shrubs in your garden.

Shrubs also include the various species of heather, which generally prefer poor, acid soil, and a light location.

A heather garden will therefore consist of plants with the same requirements. It is a common misconception that heather gardens do not need much maintenance – nothing could be further from the truth. Heathland is used for grazing

Hydrangea macrophylla *'Lanarth white'* is said to have been discovered in Lanarth, Cornwall, and grows about 1m (3ft) tall.

Left: The pinkish-red flowers of the raspberry Rubus odoratus, native to parts of North America, are borne in late summer. It likes a shady position and moist soil.

Below: Perovskia atriplicifolia has grey foliage and bears long spikes of beautiful lavender-coloured flowers in late summer. It will thrive in a sunny location.

sheep, and not simply because sheep like eating heather. Without sheep, trees would spring up all over the place in a minimum of time. Heather gardens require annual pruning for the same reason.

# CHAPTER 3

# Understanding your garden soil

The basic element of a garden is the soil in which the plants are supposed to grow. The soil's properties are therefore vitally important: its structure and humus content will determine which plants are likely to thrive in it.

If you take a good look at garden soil, you will find that it is not the same colour everywhere. It may vary from garden to garden, and from area to area within a single garden. The darker the soil, the more humus it contains. The soil may even feel warm to the touch.

*Rosa 'Mozart' bears small, single, fragrant pink flowers with large white centres. It continues flowering until well into autumn. This rose is highly suitable for naturalization.*

## *Humus*

Humus is derived from decaying plant and animal remains; it is a substance that may improve the structure of the soil. There is stable humus, and temporary humus. The former, also called permanent humus, cannot decay any further, and prevents plant nutrients being washed away. Temporary humus, on the other hand, is subject to further decay, and is a source of food for plants and bacteria.

When we consider the structure of the soil, we mean the arrangement and cohesion of its particles. Soil consists of a mixture of soil particles, and they affect its structure. Clay particles, for example, are less than 0.002 mm. in size; particles of loam are between 0.002 and 0.005 mm.

*The stemless primrose,* Primula vulgaris, *flowers in spring.*

*Next pages: This border was created on heavy soil. The green sentinels enhance its beauty.*

Particles of sand are even coarser, i.e. between 0.05 and 2 mm. Peaty soil consists of particles of decomposed plants.

The type of soil will also provide some information on its porosity and water absorption. Clay, humus-rich sand, and peaty soil can retain a lot

*Left:* Rosa *'Sanders White Rambler' is a lovely, fragrant, small-flowered rambler, and grows about 4m (13ft) tall. It flowers only once, late in the year.*

*Below:* Lavatera *'Primley Blue'*

of water, whereas poor, sandy soil is usually free-draining. You should always allow for this, not only when you are planting or replanting.

You can, of course, enrich sandy soil by adding a lot of humus or nutritive soil to it. After years of gardening and producing better soil, you will find that it contains an increasing amount of nutrients.

Ophiopogon planicapus 'Nigrescens', shown here at Sissinghurst, has handsome dark foliage.

Left: Diascias from the mountains of Natal are fairly hardy.

Below: Cornus canadensis, creeping dogwood, is a handsome ground-cover perennial for rather peaty, moisture-retentive, but not excessively heavy soil. It bears small, purple-tinged flowers followed by red berries.

## Lime-loving plants

For lime-loving species, add some powdered lime containing magnesium to the soil, or work some lime grit into the topsoil. This should satisfy the requirements of such plants. The presence of lime is usually less crucial to lime-loving plants than its absence is to acid-loving species. This means that the former will stay alive without lime, but the latter will die if the soil contains it.

Next pages: The graceful pendent spikes of flowers of Sanguisorba tenuifolia 'Alba' show up well here. The antique vase reflected in the water is also very beautiful.

Below: The floribunda rose 'Pernille Poulsen', with its lovely, pink, double blooms, goes on flowering over a long period and does not suffer from leaf fall or mildew.

## Acid-loving plants

Acid-loving plants require soil containing relatively little lime. You can use a pH-meter to determine the pH, but all you will find out is the relative acidity or alkalinity of the soil. It is better to contact one of the soil-testing establishments which will analyse a sample of your soil and give you detailed information on its nutritive condition. You can indicate the reason for your enquiry on the questionnaire sent to you. If the pH is 4 to 5, it means that the soil in your garden is acid and therefore good for growing rhododendrons and azaleas. It is generally true to say that all *Ericaceae* like slightly acid soil. If the pH is too high, these plants cannot absorb

*Chamerion angustifolium 'Stahl Rose' is the botanical name of the pink willow herb, which looks well at the back of a rather damp garden.*

*Below: The primulas belonging to the Candelabra group shown in this photograph, like growing by the waterside.*

sufficient nutrients from the soil, and will therefore turn yellow and ultimately die. The green colour (chlorophyl) is important for the photosynthesis of plants, whereas a yellow colour prevents it. If the pH is too high for this group of plants, you will need to increase the acidity of the soil. You can do this by mixing acid material such as peat in with the soil. Coniferous woodland soil will also help you to lower the pH, or you could make a mixture of well-rotted leaf mould, sand, garden peat, and garden soil.

Cerastium tomentosum *is a suitable plant for a dry spot.*

## *Sandy soil*

Sand was created from weathered stone over a period of millions of years. It is made up of large grains and has a very loose structure. This makes it difficult for the soil to retain water or to draw it up from the subsoil. Adding compost to sand improves its structure, and therefore increases its capacity to retain water.

Penstemon *'Blackbird' is a magnificent red border plant.*

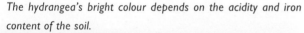

*The hydrangea's bright colour depends on the acidity and iron content of the soil.*

# CHAPTER 4

# The use of colour

Colour plays a crucial part in the effect created by plants in a garden. To make flowering plants show up to their best advantage, it is essential to choose them carefully. The impression of colour in a garden is determined by the number and type of colour combinations. The photographs of Dutch gardens in this chapter will give you some instant ideas on how to group plants, for instance, what kind of effect you might create by planting various shades of red.

*An attractive display combining the handsome daylily,* Hemerocallis, *with* Helenium *and* Acaena novae-zelandiae.

Flower shapes and types are also important when you are deciding on colour schemes. To create an attractive and varied effect, it is best to choose plants with different shapes.

Make sure that there is some colour in your garden all the year round. As winter wears on, it is the turn of early-flowering shrubs to display their wealth of colour. You should also remember to plant some of the many kinds of winter-flowering bulbs now available.

*Blue and pink make an attractive colour combination, as shown here in Els de Boer's garden in Warffum, The Netherlands.*

*Below: This yellow border with a display of* Kniphofia, Rudbeckia *and* Tagetes *may be seen at The Manor House in Upton Grey, Hampshire.*

*Yellow and white makes an attractive colour combination*

*Right: One of my favourite gardens is Church Hill Cottage Gardens in Kent, where there are magnificent borders full of colour. The photograph shows Monarda 'Donnerwolke'*

*Next pages: Rose garden in the grounds of Arcen Castle, The Netherlands.*

There are very many different kinds of colour combinations, as the garden designed by Gertrude Jeckyll at Munstead Wood will show you. Jeckyll greatly influenced the use of colour in gardens, and her style is still recognisable in famous gardens like Sissinghurst, and Hidcote Manor in the Cotswolds.

## *How plants acquire colour*

All plants, however small they may be, have some colour. The leaves and stems of most plants are green, the colour generated by chlorophylls, which, aided by light, are responsible

*This photograph was taken in the gardens of Nisse Castle. The beautiful combination of* Veronica virginica 'Rosea' *and phloxes was grown on the clay soil of the Dutch Province of Zeeland.*

*Below: The butterfly bush,* Buddleia, *attracts innumerable butterflies. The shape of its leaves is totally different from that of the cardoon,* Cynara cardunculus, *with which it forms a striking contrast.*

for the plant's food supply (photosynthesis). Without chlorophylls, plants would not survive. Several more pigments are required for the plant's metabolism, and appear when others are broken down. The foliage of some plants, for instance, changes colour in autumn, when the chlorophylls break down and red pigments are exposed to light.

The scent and colours of plants have a further significance in that they ensure that the birds, butterflies and other insects that are attracted by their bright colours or delightful fragrance will provide opportunities for reproduction.

## *The appearance of plants determines their appropriate locations*

There are several basic rules which will help you to decide where your plants will do well. Silver- and grey-leafed plants usually dislike shade. They often come from sunny regions and are best planted in full light.

Plants with golden-yellow foliage, on the other hand, do not like fierce sunlight and prefer a shady or semi-shady location, where their leaves are less likely to be scorched or to shrivel up. Ferns, too, require a dark and shady position. Plants with variegated foliage dislike nutritive soil where they would produce too much chlorophyll, thus making their leaves turn uniformly green again.

Mentha longifolia *with* Pulicaria dysenterica.

## *Designing colour schemes*

You need to bear the above information in mind when designing a colour scheme, and your choice will therefore be somewhat limited. Choosing colours for a garden is largely a matter of combining suitably matching shades with the best location for the plants. The choice of seasonal or permanent colour schemes is also restricted by the size and type of the borders. Limiting the number of colour combinations in a small garden looks better and seems more restful, otherwise it will tend to appear rather cluttered.

The amount of light also affects the choice of colours. Combinations of bright colours are most suitable in countries where the sunlight

*This red-and-white border was photographed in a model garden in Lunteren, The Netherlands.*

*Below: Ferns and hostas line this shady path near Romke van de Kaa's nursery.*

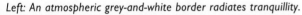

*Left: An atmospheric grey-and-white border radiates tranquillity.*

*Knautia macedonica flowers profusely in this magnificent border at the Kempenhof.*

*A monochrome colour scheme with* Coreopsis, Ligularia, Rudbeckia *and* Crocosmia.

tends to make even the strongest colours look faded. Softer shades and delicately shaped foliage, which do not stand out well in brilliant sunlight, are more appropriate for damper and darker climates, and look well in shady spots in the garden.

Growing grey foliage plants in amongst colourful flowers also helps to create a restful impression. Grey and grey-green are neutral shades, and thus tend to link the various other colours.

Make sure that groups of plants are always in harmony with their surroundings. Bright seasonal colours, for instance, look brilliant against a sober background such as a dark green hedge. Don't limit your choice to flowering plants: evergreen shrubs and those with leaves that turn beautiful colours can play a major part in your colour scheme.

*Right: Delicate shades of pink in the Cleen Lelie Gardens in Oostvoorne, The Netherlands.*

*Below: Helenium 'Moerheim Beauty' and Alchemilla millefolium 'Paprika'*

*The gardens of Sissinghurst Castle in Kent belong to the National Trust. They are full of ideas on how to combine plants and colours.*

*Pink Border*

Create quality contrasts: combine pure colours and pastel shades, for instance bright blue and old rose;
Create quantity contrasts: use a small amount of a colour to make it appear very striking;
Create colour harmonies: use two or three colours which harmonize with one another.

*Standard Rosa 'Excelsa', underplanted with Rosa 'Baby Carnival'.*

*With its warm shades of yellow, orange and red, this border is full of contrasts.*

There are several guidelines for the use of colour, but it is more important to decide on what you like and to enjoy your own garden. You may find it interesting, though, to try out some of the following suggestions:

Contrast light and dark shades of the same colour;
Contrast warm and cool colours such as red and blue;
Contrast a large area of a light colour with a small area of a dark colour
Contrast complementary colours, i.e. colours opposite each other in the colour circle;
Create successive contrasts: allow the eye to become accustomed to a colour which is retained on the retina and then combine it with a different colour.

You should also bear in mind that garden colour schemes are often viewed from a distance, when cool colours become less striking, and a subtle combination of different shades of blue soon becomes boring. A lot of mixed colours can be lovely, but the effect may also be very uninteresting.

It is also important to consider when the various plants will be in flower. If you had put a plant in a specific location just for its colour, and circumstances caused it to flower a week sooner than

you had expected, your entire scheme might fall apart, and your colour theory would not work. Always choose the colours you like – there are bound to be more than enough of them among all the available garden plants!

*A yellow-and-red border at Sissinghurst:* Ligularia vetchiana, Foeniculum, Achillea *and* Hemerocallis *'Stafford'.*

Dianthus *'Color Magician'*

Kniphofia *needs to be protected against rot rather than the cold in winter. You do this by tying the leaves together.*

## Creating a border

The following points are also important when you want to create a border containing a mixture of species:

*1.* Never make a border too small: it should measure at least 2m x 5m (6ft x 16ft). This does not apply if you want to create an attractive border in a single season.

*2.* Select a number of plants with useful characteristics such as long flowering periods, sturdiness (avoid plants that will be flattened by a breath of wind), resistance to disease, handsome foliage, and a decorative appearance after flowering.

*3.* Fill the front of the border with suitable edging plants, preferably evergreen.

*4.* Include some roses in your scheme. They look wonderful in a border and ensure that it remains colourful over a long period.

Roses are not confined to special rose beds nowadays.

*5.* If you have a long border, it is a good idea to repeat groupings of plants. This will look lovely and also restful.

*6.* It is a basic principle to plant tall species at the back of a border and low-growing ones at the front. You can then continue to 'play' with the various groups of plants. It is possible to create variety and interesting effects by introducing a tall plant, or a post with a climber growing up it, nearer to the front of the border.

*Previous pages: Veronica virginica bears blueish-mauve flowers and grows 1.5m (5ft) tall. In the photograph, it is planted next to Cephalanthus occidentalis, a handsome shrub from the swampy regions of Canada, the US, and other countries.*

*Right: A border with tall plants at the back.*

*Below: Rob Herwig's gardens include sections designed by several landscape architects. This photograph shows a yellow-and-white border.*

# CHAPTER 5

# Strong plants to cultivate anywhere

This chapter contains a list of plants that will thrive in atrocious conditions. They are not impressive to look at, and do not flower profusely; they are not very special, but they are reliable and truly faithful friends. They can withstand drought, shade, lack of care; their colours rarely clash with those of other flowers. In short, the are ideal plants for those of us who are obliged to garden on poor, sandy soil under a canopy of trees.

*Astilbes are popular border plants. They bear remarkable panicles of flowers, and will grow anywyhere.*

*It is very important to look not only at the colour of the flowers, but also at the leaf shape. The upright foliage of* Hemerocallis *looks well contrasted with the soft, lobed leaves of* Alchemilla.

*Left:* Alchemilla mollis *is a lovely plant, and highly suitable for filling gaps in the edges of a border. The leaves are far from beautiful in winter, but the abundant yellow flowers fully make up for that in spring. The plant seeds extensively.*

The lovely spring-flowering *Aconitum septentrionale* 'Ivorine' is a plant that will remain upright after a spell of autumn gales. This species of monkshood grows up to 40cm (16 in) tall and bears pretty, creamy-yellow flowers from May to July. The taller monkshoods such as *Aconitum henryi* 'Spark's Variety' are rather more difficult to cultivate as they always need staking or the support of an adjacent plant.

*Ajuga reptans*, which grows about 15cm (6 in) tall, provides good ground cover. It produces glossy, dark green leaves and bears spikes of sky-blue flower in May/June.

Attractive cultivars of *Ajuga reptans* include 'Palisander', with handsome dark brown foliage, and 'Pink Elf', which bears a profusion of pale pink flower spikes.

In several nurseries I have also seen 'Burgundy Glow', with spikes of blue flowers and silver-green leaves, and 'Catlin's Giant', which grows a little taller than the above and has larger, glossy, bronze-coloured leaves as well as spikes of blue flowers.

*Alchemilla mollis,* the common lady's mantle, is a highly decorative plant which seems at home anywhere. Its beautiful leaves are a constant joy, especially in the early morning with drops of dew on them. Abundant sprays of yellow flowers are borne from June until late August.

The cultivar *A.m.* 'Robustica' has slightly longer flowers than the species, and is very suitable for including in bouquets.

*Alchemilla alpina* is rather more demanding than the above plants. It is an evergreen perennial which has silver-grey foliage and grows about 15cm (6in) tall with a spread of 25cm (10in). It bears greenish-yellow flowers and makes excellent ground cover.

With its pale pink flowers, *Campanula lactiflora* 'Loddon Anna' shows up well at the back of a border.

*Above:* Bergenia cordifolia *has large, leathery, evergreen leaves, and is particularly suitable for planting in the corners of a border.*

With its delicate, steel-blue flowers in July and August, *Amsonia ciliata (A. angustifolia)* is another rewarding plant. It grows about 60cm (24in) tall and requires some sun, but even the shadiest garden catches an occasional ray of sunshine.

Not all Michaelmas daisies do equally well in awkward spots in the garden, but you should really give the following species a try.
*Aster divaricatus* is a genuine faithful friend, and flowers profusely from July to September. It is also very suitable for underplanting. This species grows about 50cm (20in) tall and produces small white flowers. One of its advantages is that it is still upright in the autumn, just like the large-leafed *Aster macrophyllus*, which bears a mass of pale lilac flowers from July to September. I have seen *Aster novae-angliae* 'Andenken an Alma Pötschke' still erect as late as October. This plant grows about 1.2m (4ft) tall. It requires slightly better soil than I can provide, but will then do amazingly well and continue to flower until late autumn.
*Aster frikartii* 'Mönch' is a strong and handsome ground-cover plant and probably the best known of the *frikartii* asters.

Astilbes, too, are strong garden plants. There are many different species, including both tall and low-growing kinds. The cultivar 'Bremen' is one of the 'common', but always lovely, *japonica* hybrids, genuine summer-flowering perennials. *Astilbe chinensis* 'Pumila' is a ground-cover plant.
It grows about 30cm (12in) tall and has handsome, deeply dissected dark green leaves and upright lilac-pink flowers.

*Bergenia cordifolia,* elephant's ears, will thrive anywhere – all it needs is a little sun. There are magnificent specimens available nowadays. I love *Bergenia purpurascens,* with leaves fading to red in winter and deep mauve flowers on slender stems.

*Bergenias* flower in April-May. *'Silberlicht'* is highly ornamental, but sometimes looks rather the worse for wear after the winter.
Its flowers are white at first, and turn pale pink later on.

When nothing else will grow, it is quite a revelation to see how *Calamintha nepeta* will put on an exuberant display of flowers. The bushy plant will seed everywhere, but that is far from being a disaster, since they are easy enough to pull out if it all becomes too much for you. Their maximum height is about 40cm (16in). The light blue flowers attract bees and butterflies and may be combined with anything.

You need to keep an eye on *Campanula* (bellflower), even on poor soil. Choosing the wrong species may prove a disaster. *C. persicifolia* in particular produces innumerable rhizomes which spread throughout the garden. It is preferable to opt for other species, for instance *Campanula lactiflora*.

Cymbalaria muralis

These summer-flowering plants thrive in poor soil, but not underneath trees, as they need sun. They flower for lengthy periods, a welcome bonus. They also like to have some support. One method of making them sturdier.is to cut off half their stems at the end of May, which seems very drastic, but you will find that it works. The plants will then branch out, their stems will become stronger, and more flowers will be produced.

All campanulas are rewarding plants for a border. They look well anywhere, especially when combined with plants with more attractive foliage.

You might, for instance, combine *Campanula, Lysimachia punctata* – a very strong plant – and the elegant Polemonium reptans 'Blue Pearl', which grows 30cm (12in) tall and bears blue flowers.

*C. lactiflora* 'Loddon Anna' is another well-known and lovely cultivar, with lilac-pink flowers. 'Alba', which bears white flowers, is equally beautiful. Some *lactiflora* are shorter: 'Pouffe' grows about 30cm (12in) tall, and the maxi-

Geranium macrorrhizum

Geranium oxonianum 'Rosenlicht' belongs to what are sometimes called the new generation of garden plants. Some varieties were formerly called endressii.

*Right:* Filipendia rubra 'Venusta magnifica'. This plant can grow about 2 metres (6ft) tall and bears panicles of flowers resembling candy floss.

mum height of 'Prichard's Variety' is about 60cm (24in).

*Chelone obliqua,* the turtle-head, is suitable for any soil and will grow in full sun or semi-shade. It is a delightful, sturdy plant which will flower right into autumn (from July to September). Its flowers are always a joy to look at, even in the shade. The plant grows about 60cm (24in) tall, as does the white *C.o.* 'Alba'.

As the name suggests, *Cimicifuga simplex* 'White Pearl' is a real gem for your garden. The same applies to *Cimicifuga ramosa* 'Purpurea', which flowers in September, and has a wonderful fragrance after a dry summer. It will also thrive in the shade. With its spikes of white flowers and and red leaves, this plant is highly decorative and will attract a multitude of bees.

*Unlike many plants belonging to this species,* Helleborus multifidus ssp. Bocconei *is choosy about its location. The plant comes from Sicily, central and southern Italy. As this photograph shows, it may be grown satisfactorily in a sheltered position on rather loamy soil.*

*Cymbalaria muralis*, the ivy-leafed toadflax, grows all over my garden, especially up the older walls.

The small plant looks fragile, but will tolerate considerable drought.

*Echinops*, the globe thistle, is a perennial that requires a sunny position. I have mentioned it here because it thrives on sandy soil. It grows quite tall and, with its characteristic round flower heads and prickly grey leaves, presents a decorative and somewhat unusual appearance in a border. Globe thistles are also attractive as cut flowers and for dried-flower arrangements. The flowers are borne from July to September. There are several varieties and cultivars. *Echinops bannaticus* grows up to 1m (3ft) tall and has light blue flowers that attract bees and butterflies. There are several cultivars of this *E. bannaticus* on the market. 'Taplow Blue' and 'Blue Globe' are available from many nurseries. *Echinops ritro* 'Veitch's Blue' grows about 80cm (32in) tall and is also available. As the name indicates, its flowers are blue.

*Epimedium grandiflorum* and *Epimedium* x *versicolor* are rewarding perennials. Their leaves, beautifully shaped, are slightly bronze-coloured when young.

The flowers, white, pink or yellow according to the species, are borne from April onwards, and will do particularly well if you cut off the leaves in February.

The plants are usually low-growing, about 40cm (16in) tall. I have read in a catalogue that not all species do well on clay soil.

*Eupatorium purpureum*, also known as Joe Pye weed, is a wonderful plant for poor soil. Its dark red flowers are borne late in the year, in August and September, which makes it doubly attractive.

Like the above plant, *Eupatorium purpureum* 'Atropurpureum' is rather bushy. The plants can grow up to 1.8m (5ft 10in) tall and have dark, purple stems bearing racemes of purplish-pink flowers.

For some strange reason, *Filipendula vulgaris*, dropwort, thrives in my dry garden, although it normally prefers moist soil.

This plant bears white flowers in a shady location from June until the end of August. It is a rewarding plant, if not very spectacular, with fine, deeply divided foli-age and graceful panicles of flowers.

*The vigorous* Rosa 'Bobby James' *is shown here with the ever-lovely* Rosa 'New Dawn' *and* Hosta undulata 'Albomarginata', *with its white-margined foliage.*

The cultivar *F. v.* 'Plena' has white, double flowers and, like the above, grows about 30cm (12in) tall. *Filipendula purpurea* 'Alba' and *F. p.* 'Elegans' are sturdy plants, and may be used to support those with laxer growth. *F. rubra* and its cultivars 'Magnifica' and 'Venusta Magnifica', on the other hand, often bend over under the weight of their cloudy panicles of flowers. Both species bear pink to bright pink flowers.

The familiar *Geranium endressii* with its garish red flowers will do well anywhere, so well in fact that it may need cutting back. There are also some other species of *geranium* that I can confidently recommend for awkward nooks and crannies. *Geranium macrorrhizum* is undoubtedly one of them. This is a ground-cover plant, about 30cm (12in) tall, which catches the eye even in deepest shade. There are light to deep pink cultivars, and also a white one, called 'Album' of course. These plants still look lovely after their flowers, borne in June and July, have faded. *Geranium nodosum* provides another solution for a shady spot with poor soil. Its lilac-pink flowers are borne from June until the end of September and attract many bees. The foliage keeps its looks for the whole of the season.

*Hostas were considered old-fashioned at one time, but are now very much in vogue. Some nurseries stock a good selection, including* Hosta *'Royal Standard', which bears slightly fragrant white flowers rising up above the handsome pale green foliage. This particular plant prefers a sunny position.*

*The colourful heart-shaped leaves of* Houttuynia cordata *'Chamaeleon' look well when the plant is used for edging purposes, either in a border or round a pond.*

*Geranium phaeum* is a strongly self-seeding species, hardly a drawback since it provides a little work when there is nothing else to do in the garden. I certainly would not discourage anyone from growing this plant. It bears quantities of small, delicate flowers which, depending on the cultivar, may be purple (*Geranium phaeum*); white (*Geranium phaeum* 'Album'); deep purplish blue (*Geranium phaeum* 'Lily Lovell') or purplish brown (*Geranium phaeum* var. *purpureum*).

The magnificent *Geranium oxonianum* 'Rosenlicht' is slightly more demanding. It grows about 40cm (16in) tall and its bright-pinkish-red flowers, very attractive to bees, are borne from June to September. It likes a sunny to semi-shady position and ordinary garden soil.

*Lamiastron galeobdolon 'Florentinum' looks a picture with its lemon-yellow flowers which are borne in summer.*

*Geum rivale,* or avens, is less striking, but looks lovely when combined with other plants.

It thrives on sand, but does less well on excessively moist or heavy soil. Its flowers are borne in May/June.

It is best to select a cultivar: 'Album', with white flowers; 'Leonard's Variety', which bears coppery-red flowers, or 'Lionel Cox', with warm yellow flowers.

Several species of *Helleborus* grow very successfully in my shady garden with its sandy soil. They are evergreen and have lovely glossy leaves. Because they flower so early, they really look a picture in a wintry garden.

*Helleborus orientalis,* with flowers varying from white to deep purple, is the easiest one to cultivate.

The plant grows about 40cm (16in) tall and, depending on the kind of winter, may flower as early as January. The variety 'Albus' bears white flowers, as the name indicates.

Even the stinking hellebore, *Helleborus foetidus,* is a fascinating plant. Its creamy, greenish flowers appear in panicles below dark green leaves as early as December.

The species with the largest leaves is called *Helleborus multifidus,* which has a number of subspecies including ssp. *Hercegovinus,* ssp. *Istriacus* and ssp. *Bocconei.*

*Bocconei* grows about 30cm (12in) tall and bears greenish-yellow flowers from January onwards.

*Helleborus argutifolius,* formerly called *H. corsicus* or *H. lividus* ssp. *Corsicus,* also has beautifully variegated foliage that, unfortunately, tends to be damaged in winter.

I love its magnificent apple-green flowers which, however, are frost tender. It is also a pity that you are obliged to lie down almost flat on the ground to look inside the lovely flowers of most hellebores.

While on the subject of hellebores, I should also mention the Christmas rose, *Helleborus niger.* It more difficult to cultivate than the above species, but well worth the attempt.

The plant requires semi-shade and moisture-retentive soil.

*Lysimachia ephemerum, with its blue-green foliage and white flowers, was photographed at Sissinghurst.*

Even if you are not very keen on lilies, *Hemerocallis*, the daylily, is worth trying, especially for a fairly large area in a big garden.

*Hemerocallis citrina* is genuinely worth recommending. This species grows about 80cm (32in) tall and bears small, lemon-yellow flowers in June/July. It is a strong plant, with beautiful green leaves in spring. Although the delightfully fragrant flowers only last for a day, there are usually enough buds to allow for a long flowering period.

There are also daylilies with very pronounced colours, including the brick-red *H. minor* 'Neyron Rose', and the bright yellow *H. minor* 'Stella de Oro', which looks so well combined with the difficult *Kirengeshoma palmatum*. Both of them flower in light shade until far into autumn.

Hostas, usually grown for their decorative foliage, include several species that thrive in shady positions on poor soil. Take the very ordinary *Hosta fortunei*, for instance, and all its cultivars: *albopicta*, *aureamarginata*, *hyacinthina*, and many others – they are all classic plants with handsome leaves. The colour of their flowers, however, is generally not very striking.

If you would prefer a species with beautiful flowers, then consider *Hosta clausa* var. *normalis*. This ground-cover plant has magnificent mauve flowers. *Hosta sieboldiana* is mainly attractive because of its foliage, and is, perhaps, the loveliest of all hostas. Its leaves vary in colour from grey to blueish shades. This species, too, has many cultivars, including elegans, which has very broad leaves, grows about 50cm (20in) tall, and bears lilac-white flowers. *H.s.* 'Frances Williams' is a cultivar with green-margined leaves, and prefers a shady position. *Hosta tardiana* 'Halcyon' is a low-growing, fairly new plant with lilac-pink flowers. It is worth visiting various nurseries, because now that hostas are back in fashion, there are many splendid species of this favourite garden plant available.

*Houttuynia cordata* is a handsome ground-cover plant which will spread considerably, even on

Nepeta x faassenii *is a magnificent plant for dry corners in a garden.*

*Below:* Nepeta nuda *ssp.* 'Albiflora'

dry soil; it has a tendency to become invasive. It is sometimes believed to require a moist soil. I can thoroughly recommend it as a strong plant, and I do not consider its invasiveness a major disadvantage. With its slightly heart-shaped leaves, it looks very attractive. The small white flowers stand out well against the somewhat leathery, aromatic foliage. *Houttuynia cordata* 'Plena' bears double flowers, and *H. c.* 'Chamaeleon' produces beautiful red, white and green foliage, especially in a sunny location.

*Lamiastrum galeobdolon*, the yellow archangel, is not a very remarkable plant, but it provides useful, fast-growing ground cover for a shady position. It has changed names several times. A less pretentious plant would be hard to find. A tendency to become invasive is a potential disadvantage. *L.g.* 'Florentinum' is a handsome cultivar with oval, silver-striped foliage.

Persicaria amplexicaulis *bears spikes of red flowers. There are also white, pink, and purple species.*

*Lamium*, the common deadnettle, is related to *Lamiastrum*, and is equally suitable for dry, awkard locations. The maximum height of this ground-cover plant is about 25cm (10in); it is less invasive than the yellow archangel. *Lamium maculatum* 'Album' has foliage with silvery white blotches, and bears small white flowers. The small flowers borne by *L. m.* 'Roseum' are pink, and *L. m.* 'White Nancy', produces silvery grey leaves with green margins and white flowers.

*Lysimachia*, loosestrife, is quite a different kind of plant. The best-known species is *Lysimachia punctata*, garden loosestrife. It is a handsome plant with invasive tendencies – something that is true of most lysimachias. They look especially charming in a border. I have various species and sizes in my garden, including the unusual *Lysimachia clethroides*, a fairly tall plant which grows about 90cm (36in) tall, and bears spikes of white flowers. *Lysimachia ciliata* grows a little less tall (50cm/20in) but is equally graceful, and produces fresh-looking, lemon-yellow flowers. *Lysimachia ephemerum* also bears spikes of white flowers, and looks well even when it is not in flower. The genus Lysimachia is very varied: there is also a ground-cover species, *Lysimachia nummularia*, creeping Jenny, which, with its glossy green leaves and yellow flowers, thrives in shady spots.

The genus *Nepeta,* catmint, also includes many different species. *Nepeta* x *faassenii* was formerly called *mussinii.* Now the name includes a cross, which means that the plant is a hybrid produced from two species. There are also cultivars such as *N.* x *f.* 'Six Hills Giant', a bushy plant bearing small lilac-blue flowers throughout the summer. *N.* x *f.* 'Snowflake' produces white flowers. The plants may grow 50cm (20in) tall and are useful for filling bare patches in a border. Their grey foliage alone makes them attractive for combining with other plants.
*Nepeta govaniana* bears curious tubular yellow flowers from June to September. It was formerly called *Dracocephalum govanianum* and is not

as easy to cultivate as the above species. Even so, I can thoroughly recommend it just because of its attractive flowers.

Another species worth mentioning is *Nepeta nuda* 'Ann's Choice', a plant which grows 1.2m (4ft) tall and bears pale lilac flowers in May and June. Herman van Beusekom of the 'Bloemenhoek' nursery introduced this plant and named it after his wife Ann.

Finally, Nepeta nervosa is a shorter species more suitable for small gardens. It grows about 25-60cm (10-24in) tall, bearing spikes of bright blue flowers from late July until September.

Most culinary herbs do well in my garden. That comes as no surprise since they like sandy soil and not too much moisture. They like sunshine, of course, but even that can be found in my shrubby garden. The *origanum* (marjoram) species, in fact, include a few that enjoy light shade. Neither *Origanum vulgare* 'Album' nor *O. v.* 'Compactum' grows much taller than 25cm (10in). They have aromatic foliage, and form an attractive ground-cover carpet.

Most other species of marjoram like a sunny position. They include the following attractive examples: *Origanum rotundifolium*, with lilac-pink flowers, and *Origanum rotundifolium* 'Kent Beauty' which produces pale pink flowers and pale green bracts. This herb, however, does not do too well in my garden, and I have now planted it in a pot.

I am also very fond of the handsome *Origanum laevigatum* 'Herrenhausen' with its dark lilac-pink flowers, and dark bracts. I am not the only one to love this plant – it also attracts a multitude of bees. *Origanum* flowers from June to September.

One of the well-known facts about knotweed, *Polygonum*, – which, since the publication of the new list of names of perennials, is now called *Persicaria* – is that it includes some invasive plants. Particularly bistort, *Persicaria bistorta*, has this bad reputation. Even so, I still think it is a delightful plant to have in my garden, where I take cuttings of any excess growth. I sometimes

Potentilla *'William Rollisson'*

read that the plant cannot stand soil that tends to dry out, but the soil in my garden is always dry, and I am still enthusiastic about the plant. The slender spikes of pink flowers also look delightful in flower arrangements.

*Persicaria amplexicaulis*, which bears spikes of deep red flowers, is another thriving plant. It looks particularly delightful combined with *Astilbe davidii* 'Fanal'. This plant also attracts bees and is very suitable for shady spots.

*Ranunculus aconitifolius* is a very strong buttercup with branching stems and white flowers. It grows about 60cm (24in) tall.

*Sedum,* stonecrop, can serve all kinds of purposes. This genus of succulents includes tall, low-growing, early- and late-flowering species. I shall confine myself to the indestructible kinds. First of all, there is *Sedum* 'Herbstfreude', which sometimes looks as if the cat sleeps in it. Dividing and the plant in spring and replanting it should improve the situation. 'Herbstfreude' bears beautiful umbels of deep pink flowers in autumn. It fits into all kinds of planting schemes, and is also good for flower arrangements. I think it even looks well in a wintry garden after it has finished flowering and all the flowers have turned brown. The plant grows about 50cm (20in) tall.

I once scoured the country for *Sedum maximum* 'Atropurpureum', which I had first seen growing in some gardens in England. I was given a cutting, but it failed to survive. I then visited several nurseries, and was delighted to find one eventually. Now, at last, I have several specimens of this cultivar in my garden. Everything about the plant is purplish red. It bears pinkish-red flowers in August and may continue flowering until well into October. *Sedum* 'Robustum' is a grey-leafed creeping plant which produces pinkish-red flowers in August and September.

The old-fashioned lamb's tongue, *Stachys byzantina*, also thrives in my garden. One of the properties of grey-leafed plants is that they favour dry soil, hence the fact that they are common in Mediterranean climates. This plant's flowers are insignificant; they are popular because of their felt-like grey foliage. I read in a

Stachys monieri *grows about 30cm (12in) tall and bears spikes of pink flowers in July/August.*

catalogue that *S. b.* 'Silver Carpet' often suffers from mildew, but that probably depends on its position.

*Telekia speciosa* is a very strong plant which was formerly called *Buphthalmum speciosum*. This telekia has large, bright green leaves and yellow flowers. Make sure it has plenty of room and plant it in full sun or semi-shade; its flowers will then appear like little suns from June to August.

*Thalictrum aquilegifolium* is another plant to which I am devoted. Even in winter, it still looks grand and remains upright in spite of its yellowed appearance. In summer, it produces blue-green foliage resembling that of aquilegias, and small, lilac-pink flowers. *Thalictrum aquilegifolium* 'Album' bears white flowers, and *T. a.* 'Purpureum' is a somewhat sturdier version of the common species. The plants all grow about 1 metre (3ft) tall and flower in June-July.

*Vinca major*, the greater periwinkle, makes very attractive and popular ground cover. There are several varieties. It is often classified as a semi-shrub and is not fully hardy. The lesser periwinkle, however, *Vinca minor*, is fully hardy, if a lit-

*The large yellow flowers borne by the sturdy* Telekia speciosa *are highly decorative.*

tle smaller. Its flowers are blueish mauve, sometimes light blue and sometimes dark blue. White and pinkish-white varieties are also available. I have seen a most beautiful pale blue one at a nursery, and I myself acquired a dark blue specimen, as yet unnamed, from Princess Sturdza in Normandy.

## *How and when to plant*

Everything is subject to change, and this also applies to gardens. At one time, there were strict rules on when to plant , but nowadays we are less tied to these fixed periods. The reason for this is that plants are now cultivated and sold in pots or troughs, whereas they were formerly grown in open ground at nursery gardens. When a plant was sold, it was taken straight from the earth, which frequently caused damage to its roots. That is not too serious if it happens in spring as the

plant will continue to grow. Even in autumn, root loss is no longer a major disadvantage. It is, however, the reason  why people always insisted that perennials had to be planted in spring or autumn. I will not deny that these two seasons are still the best times for planting, but, because plants are now sold in pots, it is hardly disastrous if you occasionally plant something in summer. Summer, after all, is the season when you enjoy your garden most. Because the plant's rootball is formed in its pot, and the roots are scarcely damaged when the plant is removed, you can even go on planting until the first frosts.

You should bear in mind, however, that the plant still needs looking after once it has been planted out. This means that you should water it during a dry spell. That, of course, is one of the advantages of planting in spring or autumn, seasons which tend to be damp, with moderate temperatures. All this will have a posi-tive effect on the plants' growth.

*Vinca major is a lovely ground-cover plant. There is also a cultivar with variegated foliage.*

# CHAPTER 6

# More selective plants

This chapter deals with plants that I greatly admire, but do not find easy to grow. Some of them do quite well if I devote a lot of attention to them, or if I can find a sunny spot in which to plant them. There are others, however, that I only see in gardens with better soil than mine.

Acaena novae-zelandiae *is a beautiful ground-cover plant.*
*It is good for edging purposes and for growing under tall plants.*

*Acaena novae-zelandiae* is an attractive ground-cover plant which will tolerate light shade, but does not care much for poor soil, especially if it also tends to dry out. I therefore regard it as a more exacting type of plant. It is excellent for edging purposes.

*Acanthus spinosus* is a magnificent, proud and upright plant which requires nutritive soil and a sunny position. It produces handsome, dark green leaves and pink flowers, which may be borne throughout the summer.

*Achilleas* make wonderful border plants, but do not do equally well everywhere. They thrive in humus-rich soil and like a sunny position. There are several lovely kinds, including *Achillea* 'Feuerland'.

Acanthus spinosus *looks magnificent in a large garden.*

This lovely Achillea 'Feuerland' *has reddish-brown flowers and is excellent for flower arrangements.*

*Achillea millefolium* 'Paprika' bears red flowers shading to dark yellow.
The pale-yellow *Achillea* 'Moonshine' is particularly beautiful.

*Anchusa* belongs to the cucumber family and needs a sunny location.
Unlike the related *Pentaglottis*, which spreads all over the place, this plant is more choosy about its position.
*Anchusa azurea* 'Loddon Royalist' is a plant with handsome, hairy foliage and bears flowers with colours like those of forget-me-nots.

*Anemone nemorosa* 'Robinsoniana' is a carpeting anemone with small lavender-blue flowers which likes a woodland environment.

*Anemone hybrida* 'Honorine Jobert' is a tall plant which grows to about 1.2m (4ft) and is one of the loveliest anemones that I know. One of its advantages is that it flowers late, from August onwards.

*Anemone ranunculoides* is a yellow-flowered anemone rather like a buttercup. It grows about 20cm (8in) tall.

It was in the gardens of the former home of Claude Monet, the famous Impressionist artist, that I was amazed to find *Aegopodium podograria* 'Variegata' growing as a beautiful edging plant. You may know that *Aegopodium*, bishop's weed or ground elder, is one of the most hideous weeds in existence, at least in my opinion. Not everyone, of course, will agree with me. Its variegated form, however, really looks a picture. With its creamy-white variegated leaves and insignificant flowers – best removed – it makes a lovely edging. The plant requires sun and well-drained soil.

*This yellow anemone,* Anemone ranunculoides, *is suitable for damp woodland.*

*The lovely white* Anemone hybrida *'Honorine Jobert' has beautiful foliage as well as glorious white flowers. It should be grown in a location where the soil does not dry out excessively.*

Dicentra spectabilis *looks very fragile. In fact, it is quite a sturdy plant with pendent, heart-shaped flowers.*

*Left: This tall* Anchusa azurea *'Loddon Royalist' bears forget-me-not-coloured flowers in early summer. It is a handsome plant for the back of a border.*

*Below:* Anemone nemorosa *'Robinsoniana' flowers in early spring. Afterwards, you might plant low-growing, summer-flowering bulbs in its place, or an edging of chives.*

*Aster radula is a Michaelmas daisy that is rarely seen.*

There are many beautiful species of Michaelmas daisy, but I can mention only a few here. *Aster radula* bears pink flowers and looks different from the plants that everyone else has.

*Astrantia major* 'Claret', with its dark red flowers, and *Astrantia maxima*, which bears pale pink flowers, feel at home in fairly heavy soil. That is where you will find the best forms of this masterwort.
Greenish-white or pink flower heads are produced during summer and autumn.
The plant retains its beauty after it has finished flowering.

*Ceratostigma plumbaginoides* is a plant that I have frequently lost, but because of its intensely blue flowers I have never quite given up on it. It is currently growing in a warm, sheltered spot

which has been provided with some very good soil.
The leaves turn red in autumn. The flowers produced by the small shrub *Ceratostigma willmottianum* are the same lovely shade of blue, but the plant is not fully hardy.

Most kinds of *Cirsium*, which belongs to the *Compositae* family, are weeds.
This is not true of *Cirsium rivulare* and *Circium*

*Previous pages: The flowers of Achillea millefolium 'Paprika' are a very unusual colour. It is successfully combined here with Helenium 'Moerheim Beauty'.*

*Right: I am very fond of bright blue, and therefore love Ceratostigma willmottianum. Unfortunately, this plant is rather delicate.*

*Below: This Astrantia major 'Claret' bears lovely dark red flowers. The plant does not do well in poor soil.*

*rivulare* 'Atropurpureum', a perennial which grows 1m (3ft) tall and bears its red flowers resembling pincushions on upright stems.

*Left:* Astrantia maxima

*Left, below: This sturdy plant with rosettes of leaves and crimson flowers is called* Cirsium rivulare 'Atropurpureum'. *It makes a magnificent border plant.*

*Right: I love this magnificent* Euphorbia characias ssp. wulfenii, *and I am always jealous of people who can display its splendid spikes of flowers in their gardens.*

*Below: It is said that if you hold a match to* Dictamnus albus 'Purpureus', *the burning bush, it will burst into flames, but my attempts have never met with any success.*

Nearly everyone is familiar with *Dicentra spectabilis,* bleeding heart. It is an attractive plant with graceful, arching stems and pink flowers. Cut back the leaves to just above ground level after the plant has flowered, and it will then produce new and more attractive foliage.

*Dictamnus albus* 'Purpureus', burning bush, tends to put on a disappearing act in my soil, so I have stopped buying the plant, beautiful though it is. It likes limy soil, where it will display its full beauty in June/July. This bushy plant shows up best in the middle of a border. If grown

Gaura lindheimer *flowers over a very long period. It is a fantastic plant with strong, thin stems. It is best to plant it in late spring; if you plant it in autumn, it has a tendency to disappear.*

Below: Dryas octopetala *is another attractive ground-cover plant and bears pretty cup-shaped flowers. It would be hard to tell by the foliage that the plants belongs to the Rosaseae family, though it is apparent from the flowers.*

*Geraniums have made a great come-back and are most rewarding plants. This* Geranium dalmaticum 'Roseum' *is a ground-cover plant with decorative foliage and pretty pink flowers.*

Geranium versicolor *is another attractive plant and looks well when grown at the front of a border.*

on good soil, it may be regarded as one of a basic selection of plants.

With its creamy white flowers, which are borne in late autumn and are followed by feathery seed heads, *Dryas octopetala* will provide ground cover that is unlikely to be seen in every garden.This evergreen plant produces small, oak-shaped leaves and does particularly well on peaty, stony soil.

*Euphorbia characias* ssp. *wulfenii* is a magnificent plant. In my garden, however, the slightest contretemps causes it to disappear, so I now go and admire other people's specimens.
The handsome *Euphorbia* x *martinii,* with its greenish-yellow flowers, also has more requirements than I can meet.
It is a plant that will remain upright until late autumn. Its purplish-red stems and young foliage are much admired.
It looks well combined with plants with less pronounced colours, for instance Michaelmas daisies, *Geranium nodosum* or *Geranium macrorrhizum.*

With its delicate appearance, *Gaura linheimeri* is an attractive plant to grow in large drifts in amongst other plants. It has a somewhat bushy

growth, and produces small white flowers in summer

Not all cranesbills *(Geranium)* are easy plants that will thrive anywhere. The following species will need rather more attention.
*Geranium dalmaticum* 'Roseum' requires a semi-shady position. If given some extra compost, it will provide splendid evergreen ground cover.
The plant is fully hardy, except in very severe winters.

*Another lovely geranium:* Geranium 'Brookside' *bears purple-blue flowers in summer and autumn.*

*Geranium versicolor* grows about 35cm (14in) tall and bears pale pink flowers from June to September.

*Geranium* 'Brookside' flowers from summer until autumn, bearing purplish-blue flowers. This plant grows 60cm (24in) tall and will thrive in a sunny or semi-shady position.

*Geranium sanguineum* 'Apfelblüte' is a truly lovely plant to have in a garden. Its pale pink flowers attract bees and look very well at the front of a border. Its maximum height is 20cm (8in).

*Geranium sanguineum* var. *striatum* does not grow much taller than that. All *sanguineum* spe-

Geranium sanguineum *var.* striatum *with pink flowers from* June to August.

*With its pale pink flowers,* Geranium sanguineum *Apfelblüte', is a treat for bees.*

*The lemon-yellow* Helianthus *'Lemon Queen' looks well combined with* Cornus alba *'Elegantissima'.*

cies have attractive foliage and are suitable for small areas.

*Helianthus* 'Lemon Queen' is suitable for large borders. The plants grow nearly 2m (6ft) tall, especially in nutritive soil.
They also have a considerable spread, and three plants per square metre (10 sq.ft) should be adequate.

The old-fashioned *Helenium* 'Moerheim Beauty' is a magnificent plant. Heleniums (Sneezeweed) have not been much in much demand for some time, but they have a charm of their own and flower exuberantly late in the year.

*Helenium* 'Kupfersprudel' is a handsome new cultivar bearing copper-coloured flowers on straight stems.

Some plants, including *Heuchera*, alum root, do best when grown in light shade. This is a very attractive ground-cover plant with handsome foliage.

*Heuchera micrantha* 'Palace Purple' has dark, bronze-coloured foliage and bears small white flowers on slender brown stems from May to July. I once saw these plants at Marc Brown's in France. He had planted them in an almost black border and combined them with *Ophiopogon*, which looked marvellous.

*Below: With its large yellow flowers,* Inula magnifica *'Sonnenstrahl' is suitable for an eye-catching position.*

*Inula* is a member of the *Compositae* family and bears daisy-like flowers. *Inula magnifica* 'Sonnenstrahl' has large yellow flowers; those of *Inula hookeri* have a more delicate appearance. The flowers are borne in mid summer.

The elegant *Knautia macedonica* needs a sunny position as well as good soil. Provided these conditions are met, the plant will grow anywhere. It produces a constant supply of crimson flowers

*Helenium 'Moerheim Beauty' is an old hybrid which still does very well.*

*Below: Heuchera micrantha 'Palace Purple' is a magnificent plant, especially in a sunny position.*

Helenium *'Kupfersprudel'* is often planted in borders because
its coppery flowers are borne in late summer.

*Right:* Lavatera *'Barnsley' is not fully hardy in all parts of the
country.*

with white stamens, and goes well with all kinds
of other plants.

*Lavatera*, unfortunately, is frost tender in some
parts of the country. It is more likely to survive
the winter in milder regions. *Lavatera* 'Barnsley', *Lavatera* 'Ice Cool', and *Lavatera* 'Primley
Blue' all need to be protected in winter. I read
about an interesting solution in a catalogue: take
heeled cuttings and plant them in a spot sheltered by the parent plant. The young plants are
more viable than the old one and will eventually replace their parent.

# CHAPTER 7

# Trees, shrubs and roses

Some garden lovers devote all their attention to plants. This is a pity, as so many beautiful trees and shrubs are suitable for all kinds of gardens. When you talk to people with gardens, they often turn out to be genuine plant lovers, but not very interested in trees or shrubs. Perhaps this is simply due to lack of knowledge, or perhaps they think it is all too much work, because trees and shrubs require a certain amount of attention. They need regular pruning, and most people think that must be difficult, as well as rather a shame. Still, if you don't want your garden to become overgrown, you will be obliged to wield your pruning shears sooner or later.

*This fragrant, bushy Rosa 'Mullard Jubilee', sometimes called 'Electron', is to be seen in the garden of Arcen Castle in The Netherlands.*

Trees and shrubs will usually respond to your efforts and will be more likely to put out new branches. Strange though it may seem, pruning is often better for the root system as well, since it will stimulate its development. A better network will develop underground, and that is a prerequisite for sturdy growth.

Trees are usually pruned in winter. The best time to prune shrubs is usually a matter of common sense, although there are a few basic rules. If you keep to them, you will find that shrubs simply continue to grow after you have cut off a branch or two.

## When to prune

Shrubs that flower after the first of July, bear their flowers on the same year's wood. This means that these shrubs may be pruned in March. I usually wait until the end of the month because of the continued risk of severe frost in the area where I live.

Shrubs that flower before the first of July grow on wood produced the previous year. That kind of shrub should therefore not be pruned until after it has flowered. I usually remove all the branches that have borne flowers. The plant can then start growing again immediately after the operation, and will have plenty of time to produce new branches for the following year's flowers. If the shrub produces berries after it has flowered, it would be a pity to remove all the flower branches, so, in that case, you might remove just a few branches to keep the shrub in shape.

Evergreen shrubs and conifers are best pruned in August, preferably on a slightly rainy or, at least, a damp kind of a day. Their rate of growth will be slower at that time than it is in spring, when most plants grow fastest. Box, for example,

*Right: There are different species of Malus (apple) for different purposes. Ornamental apples are grown for their flowers as well as their fruit.*

*Left: Garden in Domburg, The Netherlands.*

which will look neat and tidy for much longer if you cut it back in August rather than earlier in the year.

The larger rhododendrons and azaleas are rarely pruned. You should merely remove the occasional branch that sticks out beyond the shrub. If you have a shrub of this kind in your garden, there is very little for you to do: just make sure it keeps its beautiful shape.

The following descriptions apply to trees which do well in dry soil and shady locations.

Maples *(Acer)* are not very demanding. *Acer palmatum*, the Japanese maple, does not grow much taller than 6 metres (20ft) in north-west Europe. There are several varieties of this species, the red forms being more difficult to cultivate.

*The evergreen* Hedera helix *may be pruned into whatever shape is required.*

*Aralia spinosa* is a tree with a spiny bark. Racemes of white flowers are borne in August and attract many insects. The trees does not grow much taller than 10 metres (33ft).

Hydrangea, Buxus, *and* Matteucia struthiopteris. *Any wilted leaves of* Matteucia *should be removed regularly.*

The silver birch, *Betula pendula,* is a real pioneer on sandy soil. It has graceful drooping shoots. The tree extracts a lot of water from the soil, which makes it difficult to combine with other plants. It has a short lifespan of about fifty years.

*Carpinus betulus,* the common hornbeam, is often planted as a hedge. As a tree, it grows about 20 metres (65ft) tall.

*Ilex aquifolium,* holly, is an evergreen tree native to Europe and is often planted to provide shelter from the wind. The tree also produces berries, which makes it very attractive.

Two species of oak are native to Britain and The Netherlands: *Quercus robur,* the common oak, and *Quercus petraia,* the Durmast or sessile oak.

*The floribunda climber 'Händel' may be pruned; its branches should then be trained and tied.*

*Rosa 'Pernille Poulsen' grows about 50 cm (20in) tall and bears fairly large clusters of long-lasting flowers.*

*Right: the creamy-white* Hydrangea arborescens *'Annabelle'.*

*Rhus typhina*, staghorn's sumach, is a small tree that bears panicles of white flowers in June/July, followed by magnificent round purple fruits. Unfortunately, it also produces a large number of suckers.

*Robinia pseudoacacia*, the false acacia, is a large tree and prefers poor soil. Its branches tend to be brittle in more fertile ground. White, delightfully fragrant flowers are borne in July.

*Sorbus aucuparia*, mountain ash, is a handsome tree for poor soil and, because of its orange-red berries, a treat for blackbirds. *Sorbus aria*, whitebeam, produces red to orange-red berries and is also suitable for gardens.

Trees with beautiful bark include the following:
*Acer capillipes*
*Acer griseum*
*Betula pubescens*
*Parrotia persica*
*Prunus maackii*
*Prunus serrula*
*Stewartia sinensis*

The following deciduous shrubs are suitable for dry soil and a shady position:
*Amelanchier lamarckii*, the well-known juneberry, produces a mass of white flowers in spring. It subsequently develops fruit and, as a final bonus, its foliage colours beautifully in autumn.
Many species of *Berberis*, barberry, are fully hardy. The best-known are *Berberis stenophylla* and *Berberis thunbergii*. The latter and its cultivar *Berberis thunbergii* 'Atropurpurea' are

often grown as very inferior dividers. This is a pity, because the shrubs are very attractive, the cultivar producing more handsome, dark brown foliage.

*Lonicera,* honeysuckle, includes shrubs and climbers, deciduous as well as evergreen species. *Lonicera nitida* and *Lonicera pileata,* for example, are evergreen. *Lonicera fragmentissima* and the native climber *Lonicera periclymenum* have a wonderful fragrance.

The familiar, early-flowering *Ribes sanguineum,* flowering currant, produces pendent clusters of flowers. It will thrive in any kind of soil, in a sunny or half-shady location.

Evergreen shrubs suitable for dry soil and a shady position include the following:
*Aucuba japonica* and *Aucuba japonica* 'Variegata', both highly suitable for poor soil. The latter has variegated foliage. Aucubas prefer semi-shady locations.

*Buxus sempervirens* is a well-known hedging plant. It is evergreen, as the name indicates.

Viburnum carlesii 'Aurora'

*This lovely, fragrant floribunda* Rosa *'Westerland' adorns the Hartog Nursery in Peize, The Netherlands.*

*Cotoneaster* is available in various species and sizes. One of the best-known species is *Cotoneaster horizontalis,* at one time usually grown against the walls of houses, but now also popular for verges, where they catch all the newspapers and handkerchiefs blown away from passing cars.

*Garrya elliptica* is less familiar. This shrub can grow in dense shrubberies and woodlands. Although the plant is fully hardy, its catkins may be cut by frost.

*Hedera helix* 'Arborescens', a cultivar of *Hedera helix,* tends to dominates the winter scene in many a garden. It grows into a compact, more or less semi-spherical shape. *Hedera helix* 'Goldheart' is the self-clinging ivy that grows up walls and fences, and will ultimately cover them entirely.

*Mahonia aquifolium,* Oregon grape, bears yellow flowers in early spring, and is often grown in borders because of its glossy foliage. Its cultivar *Mahonia aquifolium* 'Atropurpurea' does not grow quite so tall and has leaves which turn brownish red in autumn. It looks particularly natural.

*Skimmia japonica* is well known for being dioecious, which means that there are male and female plants, which should be planted close together in order to produce fruit. The shiny red fruits will remain on the (female) plant for a long time.

## Roses

Magnificent roses can be grown nowadays, particularly on good soil. They are often mixed with perennials and shrubs. The modern perpetual-flowering roses are the result of hybridization and will add colour to borders over a long period. They have an abundance of beautiful foliage and lovely, informal shapes. Some bushes are rather lax and need staking. Modern roses are less susceptible to disease, which is another major improvement. The gardens of Arcen Castle in The Netherlands contain a number of these lovely plants.

# CHAPTER 8

# Plants for the patio

Bulbs are always the first plants that I mention as being suitable for growing in pots. They are very popular, as the extensive selection listed in the catalogues of mail-order firms will show. Such collections used to consist mainly of familiar names such as tulips, hyacinths and crocuses, but now many new and rare kinds are readily available. It is these modern bulbs in particular that are proving so satisfactory for planting in troughs, bowls and other containers on the patio and elsewhere.

Allium aflatuense *looks very elegant combined with new, natural-looking perennials in this border.*

Colchicum autumnale, *the autumn crocus, needs moisture-retentive, fertile soil. You may grow it indoors in a pot.*

Besides bulbs, there are many kinds of tender or half-hardy plants suitable for adorning patios and terraces. Ornamental onions *(Allium)* are among those that do very well in pots. *Allium cernuum,* for *example,* produces nodding umbels of lovely pink or white flowers; those of *Allium narcissiflorum,* also pendent, are pinkish red, and the plant's greyish green leaves are equally atractive. *Allium moly,* a yellow onion with a tendency to spread, and *Allium oreophilum,* a crimson species, are also worth planting. *Allium aflatuense,* a much taller species, does equally well in a border.

*Chionodoxa,* produces lovely blue flowers in early spring and looks particularly attractive when grown in clumps. The plants have a tendency to seed, but are also easy to weed out.

Crocuses of all kinds and sizes are a welcome addition to any garden. They emerge in spring or autumn when there is very little else in flower. They also look well in amongst ground-cover plants, in which case you are least troubled by

their unsightly dying leaves. It is worth trying them in pots as well.

Cyclamens are bulbs for autumn as well as spring. They do best in a shady position which should not be too moist. The easiest species to grow are *Cyclamen hyderifolium,* which bears pale pink flowers from August onwards, and *C. coum* which produces deep pink to crimson flowers as early as January. *C. cilicium* with its pink flowers and patterned leaves, is also worth recommending.

*Colchicum autumnale,* the autumn crocus, produces flowers on bare stems in autumn.

*Eranthus hyemalis,* the winter aconite, likes to grow in the same position year after year, preferably in soil that is not excessively dry. In a sunny position, its lovely yellow flowers will appear from January onwards.

*Right:* Eranthus Hyemalis

*Below:* Colchicum autumnale *may also be grown in the garden.*

*Erythronium*, a member of the *Liliaceae* family, is a very ancient genus.

It includes several lovely plants, for instance those of the dens-canis species (dog's-tooth violet).

There are also some lovely hybrids, including *E*. 'Pagoda', a cross between *E. tuolumnense* and *E. californicum* 'White Beauty'. Its stems bearing sulphur-yellow flowers grow 30cm (12in) tall.

The fritillaries include several species that are suitable for cultivating in containers. Occasionally, I even plant the tall crown imperial, *Fritillaria imperialis*, in a pot. The much smaller *Fritillaria meleagris*, the well-known snake's-head fritillary, is also suitable for containers. *Fritillaria uva vulpis* is less familiar; it grows about 30cm (12in) tall and has pretty, bell-shaped flowers.

Although I am not over-fond of gladioli, they still deserve a mention. They are not particularly choosy about soil, provided it is not too heavy.

If you plant the corms at a depth of about three times their width from early March onwards, you may expect flowers after an average of a hundred days.

Gladioli like a position in light shade, where their magnificent colours will show up to their best advantage.

*The magnificent sulphur-yellow flowers of* Erythronium *'Pagoda' look lovely on a patio. The plants grow about 30cm (12in) tall. Plant a few in a border as well.*

*The fritillary* Fritillaria uva vulpis *bears lovely purplish flowers on stems about 25cm (10in) tall. The tips of the petals are yellow.*

Hyacinthoides, *or* Scilla campanulata, *is a bulb which grows in British woodlands.*

*Right:* Gladiolus callianthus *in the Hortus Botanicus of the Free University of Amsterdam.*

*Hyacinthoides* is also known by other names such as *Endymion hispanicus* or *Scilla campanulata,* which is somewhat confusing. There are some other synonyms as well. In England, they are simply called bluebells, and everyone knows what you are talking about.

Every garden should contain a few irises. Most of them do not flower for very long, but their grass-shaped, pointed foliage looks well in a border of perennials.

Who can resist grape hyacinths? *Muscari latifolium* is a species that usually has a single broad leaf. This small bulb produces light blue flowers which are sometimes dark blue at their base.

*All irises, including* Iris germanica, *are lovely plants to combine in large clumps with perennials in a mixed border.*

*Narcissus* is another very familiar bulb. All kinds of narcissi are available nowadays, with flowers in every imaginable size. I often grow them in containers because they make the patio look so delightfully spring-like.

*Ornithogalum*, star-of-Bethlehem, is another genus which embraces many lovely species: from the common *Ornithogalum umbellatum*, to the magnificent *Ornithogalum magnum* with its bright-white, star-shaped flowers and yellow stamens. *Ornithogalum balansae*, with its short-stemmed flowers, is also well worth cultivating.

*Rhodohypoxis baurii (Hypoxidaceae)* belongs to a family of dwarf spring- to summer-flowering tuberous plants.

They usually have pink, red or white flowers. The plants are not fully hardy and, in a chilly climate, are therefore suitable for a greenhouse or cold-frame, or for growing in a pot which can be placed in a hole in the garden in spring.

These tuberous plants like a somewhat peaty soil mixture, which should be kept moist during the growing season. They may be propagated from seed.

When planting bulbs and corms, you should bear in mind the plants' flowering seasons. Spring-flowering bulbs should be planted in autumn.

*Previous pages: Seat with container plants.*

*Below:* Muscari latifolium *differs slightly from the common grape hyacinth in that the lower parts of the spikes of flowers are dark blue.*

*Common narcissi may be grown satisfactorily in pots.*

*There are various narcissus hybrids, including* Narcissus 'Thalia'.

*Right:* Ornithogalum giganteum *is suitable for growing in a border or in pots.*

Note the height of the bulbs. That, as a rule, is the measure for the depth of planting, usually twice to three times the height of the bulb or corm. It is advisable to plant them a little deeper in sandy soil.

Exceptions to this general rule include *Lilium candidum,* which should be planted just below the surface, and cyclamens, which should be so planted that the top of the bulbs are just visible. Do not plant bulbs or corms in places that tend to become waterlogged, as they do not like excessive moisture.

Bulbs and corms often fail to develop because of a lack of nutrients or because of shallow planting, in which case they are likely to be damaged by frost.

Bidens ferulifolia, *shown here with the vigorous Rosa 'Bobby James', may be grown in pots or in the garden.*

*Right: Trailing roses also look marvellous in pots on a patio.*

There are, of course, many other plants besides bulbs that are suitable for cultivating in pots for the patio. I grow weeping standard roses in pots and keep them out of doors all the year round, unless the winter is very severe. Half-hardy plants such as *Nerium oleander, Salvia guarantica* and *Salvia involucrata, Cassia corymbosa,* as well as many annuals flower splendidly on a terrace or patio. The problem is usually not so much their position on the patio, but where they should over-winter. It is often too hot indoors, whereas they would be cut by frost if left outside. The trick is to find a place where they are sheltered from frost and can be watered about once a week.

*Bidens ferulifolia* looks very romantic when grown in pots. This name is still somewhat unfamiliar, as this annual used to be called *Coreopsis.*

Annual petunias are still very popular. There are all kinds of beautiful forms and colours. And how about annual tobacco plants, *Nicotiana*, 'Lime Green', for instance, which has greenish-yellow flowers and grows about 45cm (18in) tall. I have also cultivated *Nicotiana sylvestris* in a pot. This species may grow about 1.5m (16ft) tall; its flowers have a wonderful fragrance in the evening.

The above suggestions show that, with a little imagination, more plants can be grown on a patio than is usually thought.

*Like all container plants,* Nereum oleander *should be taken indoors before the winter.*

*Below:* Petunia *'Sunsolos'*

**CHAPTER 9**

# Water in the garden

I do not intend to deal with the subject of ponds and bog gardens at any great length in this chapter – there are many specialized books on the subject. All I should like to do is suggest that water is a fascinating element to include in a garden, and that there are some magnificent water and bog plants.

*Right: Pond with waterlilies,* Nymphaea alba.

*Below:* Houttuynia cordata *bears small, remarkable flowers in May/June. It seems very much at home as a marginal water plant.*

*The garden of the Lenshoek, The Netherlands, harbours all kinds of idyllic spots, including this handsome woodland pond.*

*Left: pond in the Hortus Botannicus, Leiden, The Netherlands.*

All gardens are likely to have room for a little water. What is so attractive about water in a garden is that you can grow entirely different kinds of plants – plants you would never even consider otherwise. You also attract animal life, well worth while in itself. Just think of dragonflies, for instance, with their wonderful appearance and splendid colours. There are many ways of introducing water in a garden. You can make do with a water butt, and put a few water plants in it.

Another idea is to have a bird bath. Or you could opt for a genuine woodland pond. It is very restful to sit by the waterside on a summer evening and watch whatever is going on.

Some water plants grow in deep water, but have roots that need soil. It is best to plant them in small baskets which you sink to the level required by the plants. For some that is 90cm (36in), whereas others thrive in 25cm (10in) of water.

There are also plants that float on the surface, but have roots that absorb nutrients from the water. They may also be cultivated in baskets.

Water lilies, *Nymphaea alba,* are generally regarded as some of the most beautiful water plants. Even the way in which the leaves float on the water is a marvellous sight. They also provide frogs with excellent resting-places.

*Pontederia cordata,* pickerel weed, is a late-flowering plant from North America; it has lance-shaped, glossy leaves and bears spikes of blue flowers in late summer. It is fully hardy and grows about 60cm (24in) tall.

*Aponogeton distachyos,* Cape pondweed or water hawthorn, is a plant I admire, although, contrary to what is claimed in many books, it is not easy to cultivate. It grows best when planted at a depth of 40-50cm (16-20in) below the surface of

*Next pages:* Gunnera manicata, *shown here with Astilboides tabularis, needs to be covered in winter as it is not fully hardy.*

*Below: A small water spout half-concealed by ivy.*

the water, otherwise its radical tuber might be frozen into the ice. Even in winter, flowers with a delightful vanilla-like fragrance may appear.

The protected native flowering rush, *Butomus umbellatus*, may grow up to 1m (3ft) tall and requires a sunny position. Its lovely umbels of flowers appear in June and may keep their appeal well into September. Flowering rushes go remarkably well with purple loosestrife, *Lythrum Salicaria*, which may be planted either in the water or in swampy soil. This plant can grow up to 2m (6ft) tall and flowers from June to September. It is advisable not to grow it alongside invasive plants, as it will undoubtedly be squeezed out.

Marginal plants include those that prefer a moist environment, but do not always like getting their feet wet. *Gunnera manicata* from Brazil is a genuine bog plant, but it is rather difficult to cultivate. It may achieve a considerable height and spread provided it can survive the winter. For this, it definitely needs protection while it is still a young plant. A wire netting cage filled with leaves is, in my opinion, by far the best solution (black plastic is hardly a pleasant sight). Then it is simply a matter of waiting to see how it will survive the winter. Once the *Gunnera* is mature,

Polygonum campanulatum

*With its lance-shaped, glossy green leaves and purplish-blue flowers, Pontederia cordata, pickerel weed, is a splendid water plant.*

*Below: Galium odoratum, woodruff, may be grown for various purposes, for instance as ground cover at the edge of a pond.*

Lamium maculatum, *deadnettle, well known for its invasive habits, may still prove useful for awkward places.*

and has therefore grown very large, it may also be covered with its own leaves. It is a remarkable plant with large handsome leaves resem-

*The handsome* Bergenia cordifolia *is highly suitable for growing round pond edges, which it camouflages with its large evergreen leaves.*

bling those of rhubarb, and long brush-like spikes of flowers.

*Astilboides tabularis,* formerly called *Rodgersia tabularis,* is one of the *Saxifragaceae.* Like *Gunnera,* it prefers the margins of a pond. It also fits in well with the above group of plants, as *Astilboides* is not fully hardy either. Again, covering the plant with leaves is the best way of protecting it during the winter. The large round leaves look as if they are reclining on their hairy stems.

The soft rush *Juncus inflexus* is suitable for pond margins or as a bog plant. Because of their simple shape and blueish colours, these plants always look well in subtle combinations with all kinds of other plants.

*Houttuynia cordata* is a sturdy plant which may also be grown round the edges of a pond. The magnificent *Bergenia cordifolia,* a real all-purpose plant, also looks fine by the waterside.

*Water always looks peaceful, as as it does here in the gardens of Wijlre Castle.*

Use special liners along the edges of the pond. If you cover them with soil, anything planted there will create a natural transition between the water and the dry land.

Ground cover consisting of plants such as bugle, *Ajuga reptans,* or *Galium odoratum,* sweet woodruff, is best for this purpose. I have even covered a small area with deadnettles. This works well as they are very robust plants and also have pretty flowers.

# CHAPTER 10

# Propagation

Sowing, of course, is the most obvious method of propagating plants. Flowering plants usually produce fruits containing seeds. Depending on the species, the seeds may be sown when they are fresh or ripe. For sowing purposes, you firstly need good germfree seed compost of the kind that you can buy at a nursery or a garden centre with a good reputation. You also need ordinary sand, which must be clean. I often use bricklayer's sand or sand used for sandpits. Use fine gravel for drainage purposes. That is usually available at pet shops, or at garden centres selling ponds and aquariums.

*Scaevola is a lovely plant which has become very popular recently. It may be grown from seed and is very suitable for hanging baskets.*

Use clean pots, bowls, trays or pans for sowing purposes. There are plastic pots and old-fashioned red clay post.

The advantage of the former is firstly that they are easy to clean; the walls of the pot are non-porous and the remains of germs cannot therefore adhere to them. They do not need to be plunged into water beforehand to absorb moisture; they remain warmer and do not dry out as quickly as clay pots. There is of course a snag: if you water too liberally the seedlings may rot.

Use labels to remind you of what you have sown. The idea of remembering tends to be over-optimistic, and I have often found how easy it is to make mistakes.

It is advisable to have some kind of a diary in which you keep a note of when you sowed the seeds. There is a booklet which will tell you exactly how long the seeds of specific plants take to germinate. You need not keep to that exactly, as the conditions in which you sow the seeds will also affect germination. It does, however, give you some indications to bear in mind. Once you taken all these preliminary steps, you can start sowing.

You first cover the bottom of the pot with a thin layer of gravel, on top of which you put the seed compost and the sand. The pots, trays, pans, etc. should be filled to about 1cm (½ in) below their rims to allow for watering.

If the pots are to be buried out of doors, this will also prevent the seeds being washed out of the container in the event of a sharp shower. The

*Some plants are sown in autumn as they germinate in the cold.* Sanguisorbia tennifolia *is an example.*

*This Petunia 'Sunsolos' has always been popular. It may be sown in spring.*

seed should be evenly distributed, because the seedlings need plenty of space to develop once they they emerge from the soil.

The depth at which the seeds should be sown depends on their size. Very fine seed is riddled straight on to the compost, and then lightly watered with a very fine spray. Larger seeds should be covered with a layer of compost as thick as the width of the seeds. Use the same compost, but first sieve it. This top layer of compost must be dry, or the seeds will be unable to germinate because the soil is lumpy.

It is also possible to cover the seeds with very fine grit, but you only do that if you know that the seeds need more than a week or two to germinate.

The covering soil will then dry out less rapidly, and germination will be improved. After sowing the seeds, you should check regularly whether the small pots are still sufficiently moist. If not, use the same fine spray to add some water. If the plants are out of doors and it is very dry, cover them with a shading mat. It is also advisable to do something with the pots if the event of a long rainy spell. You can either take them indoors, or put them in a frame or a greenhouse. Otherwise, you may find that all your efforts have been in vain and that the pots contain nothing but rotted seeds.

As soon as the seedlings come up and are large enough, you may start pricking them out. Use a slightly larger pot or other container for this pur-

pose, and allow adequate space between the plants.

I always use wooden labels for pricking out, and cut notches at one end. I use one label to lift the plant out of the soil and the one with the notch to hold the small plant. Make a small hole in the compost, and simply slide the seedling into it. Firm the plants in, so that their roots are in contact with the compost and there is no chance of their drying out. Then they can begin to develop a rootball. If some of the seeds still have not germinated after you have been watching them anxiously for a long time, bear in mind that some plants will only germinate after a cold spell. That kind of seed may quite well be left out of doors for another year. If they ultimately fail to produce anything, they can always be thrown away then.

*Lavatera 'Barnsley' may also be grown from seed.*

## *Division*

It is very simple to propagate plants by dividing them. Remove the plants from the soil and split or cut them into sections, making sure that each piece has some roots. The method does not, of course, apply to plants with tap roots. Each of these plants has a long single root, whereas others produce a mass of them.

Plants with tap roots are difficult to transplant for the same reason. The best times for dividing plants are spring and autumn, just as they are for planting.

Plants that flower early in spring may be divided immediately after flowering, but it would be better to wait until autumn.

Autumn-flowering plants are best divided in spring. If you divide them too late in the year,

*Euphoriba characias ssp.* wulfenii *may be propagated by division.*

*Monarda 'Beauty of Cobham' may also be divided.*

they may not establish themselves before the frost, and will therefore die. Plants that have been divided are usually replanted in the same place, but if you are at all afraid of losing them for some reason, it is also possible to put them in pots first and wait until you are sure that they have become established.

## *Cuttings*

Taking cuttings is another method of propagation. You will need a special cuttings compost for this purpose. Its composition may vary, as people tend to develop their own favourite mixture. Usually it consists of sand and peat dust, a pleasant and airy mix. Use it to fill the trough or pot in which you intend to plant the cuttings. Cover the containers with a sheet of glass or a plastic bag, and stand them in a warm place out of the sun.

The small indoor propagators consisting of two plastic trays are also very useful. One of them is translucent and is used to cover the cuttings. If they are covered, the soil will remain moist and humidity will be high, so that the cuttings stand a better chance of developing roots.

There are rooting powders and liquids available which make it easier for the cuttings to take root, but it must noted that they have little effect on some plants, and may even damage them. So it is really best to try them out first.

Of course there is no need for you to reinvent the wheel – there are all kinds of booklets available in which the various methods of propagation are clearly explained.

## Stem cuttings

Stem cuttings may be taken immediately after the plant has flowered, or else in October/No-

*Nerium oleander 'Rosa Semplice' is easy to propagate from cuttings, which will even root in water.*

vember. These may be called half-ripe or fully ripe cuttings respectively. Stem cuttings are generally taken from plants that do not produce seed, or are not true to type if grown from seed. This method is also suitable for plants that are naturally difficult to divide.

Tip or soft cuttings are taken immediately after the plant has flowered, usually in July/August, when the shoots are strong enough but not too hard.

Use a sharp knife to cut them off diagonally just below a leaf-joint and remove the lowest leaves. Dip the cutting in rooting powder or liquid if you wish. Shake them to remove any excess powder of fluid. Then insert the cuttings in the cuttings medium and cover with the sheet of plastic or glass.

Fully ripe or hardwood cuttings are placed in a cold frame or greenhouse and covered with a rush mat or insect screen. If there is no frost, the covering material may be removed and the con-

*You may propagate* Aubrietia deltoidea *by taking cuttings in August and September, or by dividing the plant in autumn.* Aubrietia *may also be sown in March.*

*Below: Shrubs such as* Hydrangea arborescens *'Annabelle' may be propagated by means of cuttings.*

tainer aired. The cuttings often manage to grow roots during the winter.

Tip cuttings are cuttings taken early in the year from the growing ends of the plant's shoots. They are cut off diagonally just below a leaf-joint. The lowest leaves should be removed, as they tend to rot in the cuttings medium.

Their further treatment is the same as for other stem cuttings.

## Heel cuttings

Cuttings from a number of plants, especially woody kinds, should be taken from somewhat older wood. Hardwood cuttings of this kind are taken from sturdy one-year-old stems, but there are also some which do well when taken from two- or even three-year-old wood. To obtain a heel, the cuttings are not cut, but pulled off the plant, when a small piece of older wood comes away with the cutting. Trim the heel slightly to prevent it rotting in the soil. Make a hole in the cuttings medium and insert the cutting. This method is adopted mainly for plants from which it is difficult to grow cuttings in spite of the use of a growing medium and a plastic cover.

## *Layering*

Layering is quite a different method of propagation. Bend a stem over to touch the ground, either directly or by means of a series of bends. Place a weight, for instance a stone, on the tip of the stem, which will then develop roots underneath the weight. As soon as there are enough roots, cut off the branch. You can then plant the section with the roots wherever you wish, and this will become a new shrub.

If the stems are very pliable, you can try the following procedure: cover some, but not all, sections of the stem on the ground with soil or stones. Do this in early spring. At the end of the growing season you will be able to remove the shoots along with their roots and then plant them.

*Lavatera 'Ice Cool' is a plant from which you should take cuttings with a 'heel'.*

*Young shoots of Wisteria sinensis are fairly easy to layer.*

# Pests and diseases

Diseases and infestations are unpleasant subjects to write about, but, unfortunately, they cannot be avoided when you are dealing with gardens. A weak and sickly plant is more likely to be stricken than sturdy plants that are doing well. I am thinking in particular of fungous diseases which tend to affect plants that are not good at withstanding our damp winters. There are remedies, but the real skill lies in recognizing the disease at an early stage. In damp periods, the fungi spread from plant to plant by means of their spores, and a whole series of plants may be afflicted in less than no time.

*One of the lovely Priona Gardens at Schuinesloot in The Netherlands is especially designed to attract butterflies.*

Snails love Primula vulgaris (primrose). You can, of course, use snail pellets, but half-buried jars of beer are worth trying.

Left: Rosa 'New Dawn' is quite frequently affected by mildew, particularly during periods of drought. Mildew looks like a powdery deposit on leaves and shoots. There are various commercial remedies for this fungus infection.

Animal pests may also be a nuisance in our gardens. To me, snails are among the worst. They are capable stripping entire plants. It is possible to get rid of them by scattering slug pellets amongst the plants. This really means killing them with a pesticide, something I tend to dislike. I prefer them to be eaten by birds, toads or hedgehogs. In wet summers, however, there are a great many snails and slugs.

Birds are sometimes a nuisance as well, because they churn up entire areas in search of food. I try to catch as many snails as possible in jars of beer half-buried in the soil, where they come to a drunken end. I also make sure that there are several berry-producing shrubs in the garden, so that the birds have no need to start eating my plants.

Although butterflies usually look lovely, they may also do harm in the garden. They rapidly lay their eggs on the undersides of leaves, and the larvae are even quicker at stripping your plants bare. Quite early in the season, the charming cabbage white and brimstone butterfly will be about in search of phloxes and aubrietias where they can begin their destructive work. In summer, there are creatures such as hawk-moths that regard your deliciously fragrant pinks as their favourite food. As soon as I see butterflies, I go round the garden to see if there are any small eggs attached to the undersides of the leaves. I remove those leaves, and in that way I have butterflies, but not so many plants that have been stripped of their foliage.

Aphids, too, may be active in the garden, although they usually affect only a few of the many different plant species contained in an average garden. Still, plants cease to look very attractive

Delphiniums, this Delphinium 'Ouverture' for instance, are also subject to attack by snails. They may also be affected by mildew.

when they are covered with aphids, so you will be obliged to take some action. The days of washing the plants down with soapsuds and meths may be past, but you can still remove quite a lot them by holding a cloth round a stem and moving it upwards from the base. There are also selective insecticides, which provide an easy method of tackling the aphids.

Moles are attractive and usueful creatures because they eat some of the insects that attack your plants. Even so, they are a nuisance in the garden. They literally turn everything upside down, which is hardly what you want after all your efforts. Catching a mole is not easy. You can set traps, but I think that is a horrid method. You can also lie in wait for them with a spade in

Claytonia sibirica

*Below: Roses are often invaded by aphids. Rosa 'New Dawn' may also be affected in this way.*

*Provided they are planted in suitable locations, Euphorbias are scarcely subject to disease.*

*Passion flowers, including Passiflora caerulea 'Star of Mikan' are often invaded by insects which eat their leaves.*

the early morning. There are several so-called tricks for getting rid of moles, but not one of them has worked for me. All I can say is: 'Be glad you are troubled with moles, because that means you have a garden, and a slightly rural one at that.'

Apart from these tiresome creatures, there are also some that we like having about in the garden. I'm thinking of bees in particular. It is a splendid sight to watch them enjoying the nectar so abundantly available in early and later flowers. Sedums, salvias, *Cotoneaster,* and many other plants ensure that large numbers of these insects feel at home in our gardens.

# Index

# Acknowledgements

The author would like to thank the following photographers, garden owners and nurseries.

**Photographers**: Martina Hop, Maya Roozen and Nico Vermeulen, all of Groningen, The Netherlands

**English gardens:**
Bateman's Cottage, Burwash, East Sussex
Church Hill Cottage Gardens, Charing Heath, Kent
The Courts, Holt, Wiltshire
The Manor House, Upton Grey, Hampshire
Nymans Garden, Handcross, West Sussex
Sissinghurst Castle Gardens, Sissinghurst, Kent